The Big Fat Book of Hillary's Top Ten Accomplishments!

And other cool stuff

The Shortest Book Ever Written!

By

Dr. Leonardo Enoch Bonobo

Master of the Universe and Much, Much More

Copyright 2015 1-2562123921

ISBN 13:978-1515122395 ISBN 10:1515122395

The Wise Dr. Leonardo Enoch Bonobo

DEDICATION

This book is dedicated to the long forgotten tradition of Truth, Justice, Laughter and the American way! And, to my mentor Dr. Zaius and Yoda.

Let it be said, let it be written!
Somebody said that? Right?

Believe this stuff or not. If your panties get wadded up and you walk like a penguin, Dr. Leonardo Enoch Bonobo doesn't care. This is politico satire. Deal with it!

Introducing
The Distinguished
Board of Directors of
The
DNCC
Democrats National
Corruption
Committee

Mr. Al Capone, Esquire
Founder & Chairman

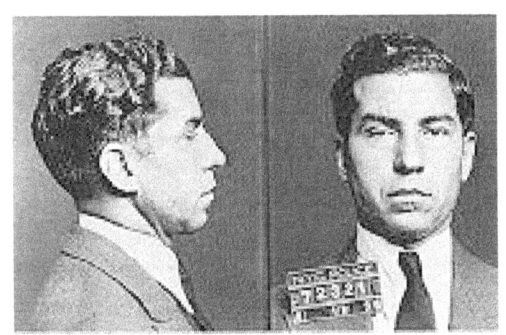

Dr. Charles Luciano
"Lucky"
Vice Chairman and Director of By-Laws

Dr. Meyer Lansky
President and Director of Fundraising

Dr. Frank "the Prime Minister" Costello
Vice President of Government Relations
and Bribes

Dr. Carlo Gambino
Vice President of By-Laws Enforcement
and Legal Affairs

Dr. Benjamin Siegel
Vice President of Public Relations and
Good Time Acquisitions

Remember, the DNCC demands that you;
"Vote Early. Vote Often. Vote, even
if you're dead."

That's the Chicago Way!

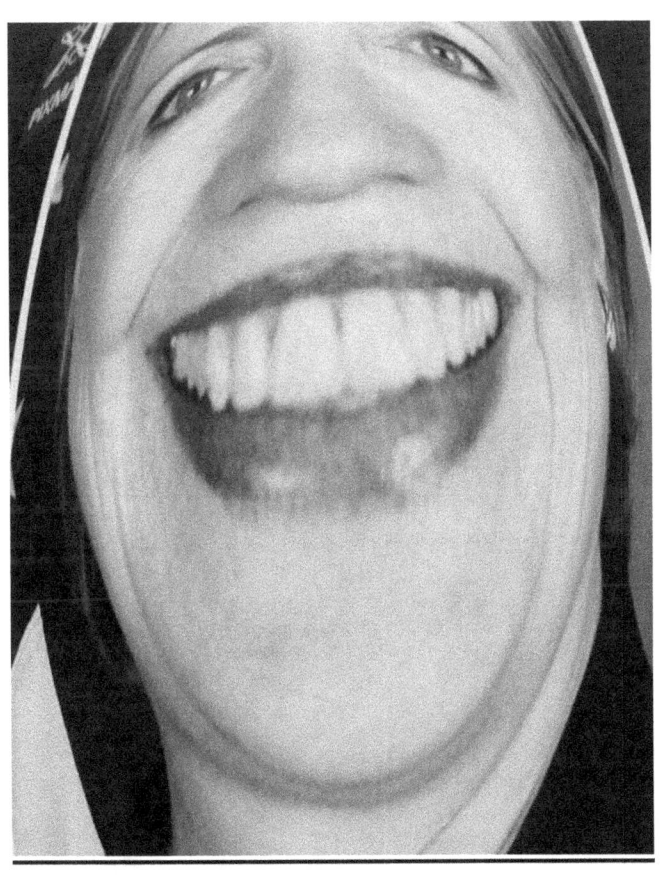

I want to be your champion!

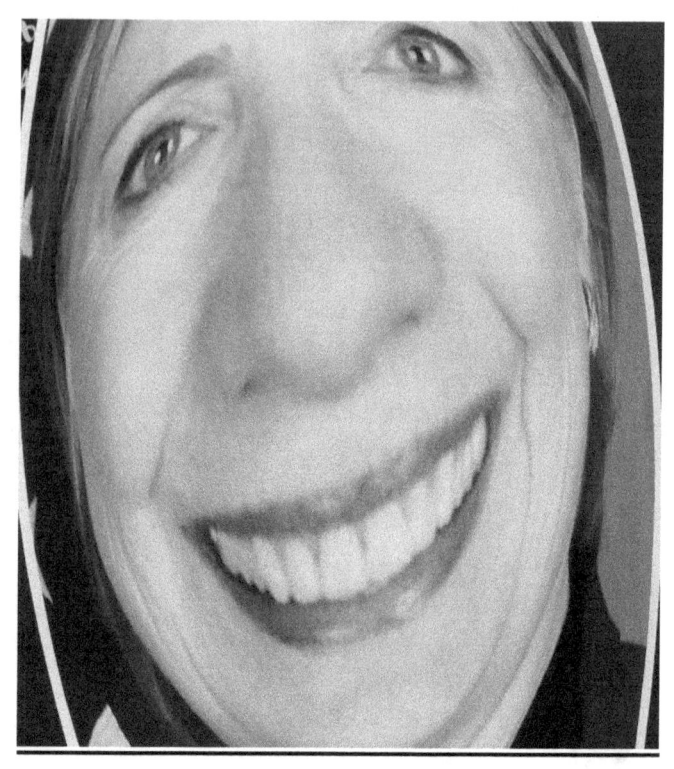

Remember, I'm a champion
and not a liar! Right?

ACKNOWLEDGMENTS

I hereby acknowledge myself-- the Great Dr. Leonardo Enoch Bonobo, my goldfish, really good pizza, that big red dog down the street, scratch less toilet paper, roller skating monkeys, baby back ribs, kettle chips and great whiskey! Oh yeah, and the wisdom of politicians.

I also wish to thank Hillary for being the most transparent politician since

Barack Obama. In order to demonstrate her transparency to America, while serving as Barack Obama's Secretary of State, she installed a private Internet network server in her home, used her private email address for government business, then erased thousands of emails and refused to turn over the network server allowing unbiased experts to examine its contents for official government emails and national secrets. Now, if that isn't transparency, Dr. Leonardo Enoch Bonobo doesn't know what is?

Well, as her husband Bill Clinton testified under oath before a Federal Grand Jury regarding his sexual relations with one of his White House interns,

"It depends upon what the meaning of the word 'is' is."

So I guess it depends on what the meaning of Transparency is?

Now that clears it up!

OOPS!

Dr. Leonardo Enoch Bonobo Almost Forgot to Mention this Little Gem.

On December 19, 1998, President William Clinton was **impeached** by the **House of Representatives** on two charges, one of **perjury** and one of **obstruction of justice** as the result of his Grand Jury Testimony.
OUCH! That wasn't good!
But fear not, the democrats loved the guy so much they endorsed his perjury and obstruction of justice by not voting to remove him from office.

Mr. Al Capone, Esquire

After the vote which saved Bill Clinton's behind, the NDCC founder and chairman Mr. Al Capone, proclaimed on the steps of the Capital, surrounded by cheering democrats from the House of Representatives and U.S. Senate,

"I'm all for Perjury, Obstruction of Justice and Transparency in Government! This is the best Congress money can buy! Now, how many of you democrats want another bribe? I mean donation!"

THIS IS WHERE THE TABLE OF
CONTENTS WOULD BE, IF THERE
WAS A TABLE OF CONTENTS.

Dr. Leonardo Enoch
Bonobo

THIS WAS A BLANK PAGE UNTIL I, Dr. Leonardo Enoch Bonobo, TOLD YOU IT WASN'T.

Oh No! Another Blank Page

Last Blank

The Fable Begins

Once upon a time, in a galaxy far far away---somewhere west of Tightsqueeze, Virginia, there was a timeworn lady who accomplished so darn much, that earthlings worshiped at her feet, fainted at the sound of her voice and erected shrines to her ever expanding elastic waistband pant suit! Not to mention the tons of incense they burned at their bizarro pant suit shrines---polluting the air, melting the glaciers and irritating playful dolphins and cute little puppies to no end!

And they caused mother earth to weep from the soot wafting into her majestic eyes from those stinking incense burners.
Dorothy this is not Intercourse, Pennsylvania, this is America. But it could be.

HILLARY'S TOP TEN ACCOMPLISHMENTS THE COUNT DOWN BEGINS!

HER TENTH BIG FAT ACCOMPLISHMENT!

?

HER NINETH BIG
FAT
ACCOMPLISHMENT!

?

HER EIGHTH BIG
FAT
ACCOMPLISHMENT!

?

HER SEVENTH
BIG FAT

ACCOMPLISHMENT!

HER SIXTH BIG FAT

ACCOMPLISHMENT!

?

HER FIFTH BIG FAT ACCOMPLISHMENT!

?

HER FOURTH BIG FAT ACCOMPLISHMENT!

?

HER THIRD BIG FAT ACCOMPLISHMENT!

SHE'S NEVER TOLD A LIE!

YOU BETCHA!

HER SECOND BIG
FAT
ACCOMPLISHMENT!
<u>NO KIDDING!</u>

PUTTING STYLE IN THOSE EVER EXPANDING ELASTIC WAISTBAND PANT SUITS!

HER NUMBER ONE
AND MOST
PROFOUND,
BIGGEST AND
FATTEST
ACCOMPLISHMENT
EVER!

NEXT PAGE

DELETING THOUSANDS OF EMAILS!

YEAH BABY!

WE BELIEVE YOU!

NOW THE OTHER COOL STUFF

IN CLOSING, A FEW ASTUTE WORDS FROM THE MOUTHS OF POLITICANS

(YOU CAN'T MAKE THIS STUFF UP)

Joe Biden

"I'll tell you what, there's never been a day in the last four years I've been proud to be his Vice President, not one single day. Not one single day." **Joe Biden** November 2, 2012

"I've had a great relationship. In Delaware, the largest growth in population is Indian-Americans moving from India. You cannot go to a 7-Eleven or a Dunkin' Donuts unless you have a slight Indian accent. I'm not joking," **Joe Biden** 2006

"first mainstream African-American who is articulate and bright and clean and a nice-looking guy."
Joe Biden 2007 said that regarding Senator Barack Obama

*"Neal Smith, an old **butt** buddy. Are you here, Neal? Neal, I miss you man. I miss you."* **Joe Biden** February 12, 2005. WTF does that mean?

"This is a big fucking deal!" **Joe Biden** said to Barack Obama on passage of Obamacare.

Richard Nixon

"If the President does it, it's legal." **Richard Nixon** 1977

"I am not a crook!" **Richard Nixon** 1973

George W. Bush

"Too many OB-GYNs aren't able to practice their love with women." **George W. Bush** September 2004

"I know the human being and fish can coexist peacefully." **George W. Bush** September 29, 2000.

Jimmy Carter

"I've looked on a lot of women with lust. I've committed adultery in my heart many times." **Jimmy Carter** 1976 Playboy Magazine.

Hillary Clinton

"You have no reason to remember, but we came out of the White House not only dead broke, but in debt," Clinton said. "We had no money when we got there, and we struggled to piece together the resources for mortgages for houses, for Chelsea's education." **Hillary Clinton 2014**

Dr. Leonardo Enoch Bonobo finds her "broke" statement puzzling. It's been reported that upon leaving office, her husband Bill Clinton received a pension of $210,000 per year for life. That's four times the average medium household income. And, he received hundreds of thousands of dollars per year to support his personal office. They also purchased two homes; one in Chappaqua, NY for $1,700,000 and another on Embassy Row Washington, DC for $2,850,000 totaling over $4,000,000.00. If that is broke, broke is a good thing. Perhaps that "concussion" deleted her memory.

"Who is going to find out? These women are trash. Nobody's going to believe them." *She ranted in 1992 referring to women Bill was accused of having an affair with.* I guess she is a champion for women, right? **Hillary Clinton**

"We are going to take things away from you on behalf of the common good." **Hillary Clinton** 2008.

"We have a lot of kids who don't know what work means. They think work is a four-letter word." **Hillary Clinton** 2008.

"If I didn't kick his ass every day, he wouldn't be worth anything." **Hillary Clinton** referring to Bill Clinton.

"I suppose I could have stayed home and baked cookies and had teas, but what I decided to do was to fulfill my profession which I entered before my husband was in public life." **Hillary Clinton** during Bill Clinton's 1992 campaign.

"I believe that marriage is not just a bond, but a sacred bond between a man and a woman"…… " the fundamental bedrock principle that marriage exists between a man and a woman, going back into the midst of history as one of the founding foundational institutions of history and humanity and

civilization, and that its primary, principal role during those millennia has been the raising and socializing of children for the society into which they are to become adults." **Hillary Clinton** speech to the US Senate 2004. Really?

"I remember landing under sniper fire. There was supposed to be some kind of a greeting ceremony at the airport, but instead we just ran with our heads down to get into the vehicles to get to our base." **Hillary Clinton** March 2008 regarding her 1996 visit to Tuzla, Bosnia. OOPS! There were no snipers and days later she retracted the statement stating she "misspoke."

During an 1998 interview with Matt Lauer of NBCs *The Today Show*, Hillary discussed Bill Clinton's affair with White House Intern Monica Lewinsky, **Hillary Clinton** said this;

"This is—the great story here for anybody willing to find it and write about it and <u>explain it is this vast right-wing conspiracy</u> that has been conspiring against my husband since the day he announced for president. A few journalists have kind of caught on to it and explained it. But it has not yet been fully revealed to the American public. And actually, you know, in a bizarre sort of way, this may do it."

Yes, in a bizarre sort of way, it did do it!

The interview continued……..

LAUER: Let me take you and your husband out of this for a second. Bill and Hillary Clinton aren't involved in this story. If an American president had an adulterous liaison in the White House and lied to cover it up, should the American people ask for his resignation?

Hillary CLINTON: Well, they should certainly be concerned about it.

LAUER: Should they ask for his resignation?

Hillary CLINTON: <u>Well, I think that—if all that were proven true, I think that would be a very serious offense.</u> That is not going to be proven true. I think we're going to find some other things. And I think that when all of this is put into context, and we really look at the people involved here, look at their motivations and look at their backgrounds, look at their past behavior, some folks are going to have a lot to answer for.

Interesting, the evidence proved otherwise.
Who knew!
Dr. Leonardo Enoch Bonobo.

"The only Ben Ghazi I know is a gay porn star. Besides, what difference does it make?" **Hillary Clinton.** Dr. Leonardo Enoch Bonobo dreams she said this.

"Pandering for votes? I would never do that. I simply promise everyone, including illegals, everything they ever wanted and the government will pay for it. Yeah,

that's the democratic ticket! Socialist rule!" **Hillary Clinton**. Again, Dr. Leonardo Enoch Bonobo dreams she would say this.

Bill Clinton

"I did not have sexual relations with that woman, Miss Lewinsky." **Bill Clinton** January 26, 1998

Really Bill?

OOPS!
He was impeached for this stuff. I guess he forgot!

Here's a little passage from **page 18 of the Official Kenneth W. Starr Independent Counsel Report Sept 11, 1998**

According to Ms. Lewinsky, she performed oral sex on the President on nine occasions. On all nine of those occasions, the President fondled and kissed her bare breasts. He touched her genitals, both through her underwear and directly, bringing her to orgasm on two occasions. On one occasion, the President inserted a cigar into her vagina. On another occasion, she and the President had brief genital-to-genital contact.

Whereas the President testified that "what began as a friendship came to include (intimate contact).

OOPS!

As many have said, the Truth hurts! I wonder where he obtained that *Right Wing Conspiracy Cigar* or R.W.C.C.?

Nancy Pelosi

"It's going to be very, very exciting," Pelosi *giggled telling elected buffoons and reporters assembled before her that Congress* **"has to pass the bill so you can find out what's in it…….."** **Nancy Pelosi.**

"Let me understand her logic; they pass a bill without knowing what is in it? As the prominent primate psychiatrist evaluating the lack of the most basic primitive mental capabilities of politicians, this bizarro statement is not surprising. It is emblematic of all who voted for Obamacare. If politicians ran their life in this manner, they'd still be living in caves; marvel at fire and my relatives would be hanging out in trees instead of lecturing at Universities."
Dr. Leonardo Enoch Bonobo

Harry Reid
*" a 'light-skinned' African American 'with no
Negro dialect, unless he wanted to have one,'*
Harry Reid comments on Barack Obama.

Barack Obama

*"No, no. I have been practicing...I bowled a 129.
It's like -- it was like Special Olympics, or
something."* **Barack Obama** "The Tonight
Show," March 19, 2009

"... it is just wonderful to be back in Oregon, and over the last 15 months we've traveled to every corner of the United States. I've now been in fifty .... seven states? I think one left to go. One left to go. Alaska and Hawaii, I was not allowed to go to even though I really wanted to visit but my staff would not justify it." **Barack Obama** May 2008, Beaverton, Oregon.

"My position hasn't changed" on using executive authority to address immigration issues." **Barack Obama**, November 2014. Okay, so he lied again? You can't toss him out of office! Suckers!

"if you like your health care plan, you can keep your health care plan" **Barack Obama**

Dr. Leonardo Enoch Bonobo

"When politicians flap their lips, it gets deep and I need my boots." **Dr. Leonardo Enoch Bonobo**

"Politicians didn't invent lying. They've turned it into a career." **Dr. Leonardo Enoch Bonobo**

REMEMBER THESE WORDS

"THERE ARE A NUMBER OF WAYS TO DESCRIBE MAJOR POLITICIANS AND THEIR STATEMENTS, THESE ARE JUST A FEW; LIES, UNTRUTHS, FALSEHOODS, FIBS, INVENTIONS, PROPAGANDA, DECEIVER, STORYTELLER, FIBBER, PERJURER, FALISFER, HYPOCRITE, PHONY, CHEAT, FRAUDSTER, CON ARTIST, PREVARICATOR, SNAKE OIL SALESMAN, SWINDLER, FAKE, BULL SHITER, CHARLATAN AND MY FARVOITE, "CONFIDENCE TRICKSTER."

DR. LEONARDO ENOCH BONOBO

And remember,
liar, liar, those
big fat ever
expanding
waistline pant
suits are on fire!

The symbol of the Democratic Party is
the well-earned Jack-Ass.
Stubborn and Stupid.

As a highly respected psychiatrist Dr.
Leonardo Enoch Bonobo ask; will you
continue to be a Jack-Ass?

SWEET DREAMS LITTLE MONKEYS

"Lying, inept and corrupt politicians can only be elected when a person is so friggin' stupid they believe their BS and vote for them. Are you that stupid? Again?"

Dr. Leonardo Enoch Bonobo

The End